MW00711812

HIDDEN
MESSAGES
OF
HOPE

John Carroll

First published in 2017
by Eyewear Publishing Ltd
Suite 333, 19-21 Crawford Street
Marylebone, London W1H 1PJ
United Kingdom

Cover design by Ray Geier I squishiepuss.com
Layout by Brian Manley I funwithrobots.com
Author photograph by Wes Cummings I wesleycummings.com
Edited by Matt DeBenedictis and Jessica Hunt
Printed in England by TJ International Ltd, Padstow, Cornwall

All rights reserved
© 2017 John Carroll

The right of John Carroll to be identified as author of
this work has been asserted in accordance with section 77
of the Copyright, Designs and Patents Act 1988

ISBN 978-1-911335-75-7

*Eyewear wishes to thank Jonathan Wonham
for his generous patronage of our press.*

WWW.EYEWEARPUBLISHING.COM

Ryan,

Keep the Hope Alive!

INTRODUCTION

Six years ago I was going through an extremely difficult time. My personal life was in turmoil and my job made me miserable. My heart was broken. It took everything within me just to get out of bed in the morning. It seemed like a miracle that I got through each day. For the first time in my life, I knew what depression was.

Every night before I went to bed I'd stare myself down in the mirror and say, *You're going to get through this. Just hold on.*

Bored at work, I would search the Internet looking for anything to distract me. That's when I first discovered blackout poetry, via the work of Austin Kleon.

I started making homemade postcards with blackout messages on them to send to my friends and family. After a few of the postcards were stolen or destroyed by postal workers ripping them apart to get the messages, I decided to just make the blackout poems and skip the post office altogether.

Night after night, I sat at my kitchen table with a Sharpie and used anything I could get my hands on that had any kind of text to turn out blackout poems. I'd frame them and give them to friends, but mainly I just piled them up and got started on the next one.

The messages were dark and grim, usually revolving around depression and psychosis, but they helped me process my pain. I made blackout poetry for the better part of a year until I finally got my head back on straight. Another year went by before my friends started making comments about my blackouts, encouraging me to create more of them.

I kicked the idea around in my head for a few months, until one day I found myself at an art supply store. While standing in the checkout line I decided to buy some black, white and red acrylic paint to see if I could reimagine what I had done the previous year in terms of blackout poetry. Sharpie markers weren't cutting it anymore.

I've always considered blackout poetry an exercise for the subconscious mind and was surprised to find that my poems no longer focused on despair and depression, but hope and passion.

My love for creating blackout poetry was revived. And though I had never painted a day in my life, I couldn't put down the paintbrush. I was addicted.

As the first few weeks went by I found myself encouraged by what I was painting. Messages of truth and hope filled the pages as I painted blackout after blackout. From there I made the decision to not only share my blackout poetry with friends and family, but to make it public for everyone.

As social media has risen in popularity, I noticed how self-centered we've become as a generation. Not only that, I could see the destructive nature of the masses—not to mention a lot of people hurting out loud.

My goal was to combat the negativity that fills pages and pages of the Internet by offering hidden messages of hope and compassion to everyone who would take the time to stop and read.

I decided to be anonymous in presenting the art, so that no one would be swayed by my gender, race or personality.

'You can kill a man, but you can't kill an idea.' — Medgar Evers

I didn't create blackout poetry, I'm just another person who decided to give it a try. I also wanted to encourage others to make blackout poetry: I didn't want this to be about me, but I wanted it to be about us.

Humanity.

People.

Taking one step at a time to complete our journeys.

So though I may own the website and post on the Instagram account, everyone who makes blackout poetry is another individual who has chosen to create something that is honest and personal and can make an impact on the world. They've become more than a person, they've become part of the idea.

When I created the Instagram account, my goal was to post a blackout poem every day for a year as a challenge to myself. In April of 2014, I completed my first year of blackout poetry, with over 400 blackout poems created by myself and others.

Make Blackout Poetry is now over four years old, and it has evolved. I am no longer alone in this endeavor, but surrounded by a community of like-minded creatives who spread truth and hope in our little corner of the Internet.

I am constantly blown away by the love, support, encouragement, and creativity of the community that has formed around this.

For those of you who make up this community: Thank you for every comment, 'like', share, retweet, reblog and every time you decide to make blackout poetry. Without you I would still be sitting at my kitchen table putting my poems in a pile. You've truly made this a beautiful experience for me. I hope I've done the same for you.

If blackout poetry is new to you, I invite you to join us. It's your choice to be a creator or a spectator, but I hope after reading this book you'll take the plunge and make your own.

PASSION

'You don't have to be boring.'

Why do you wake up in the morning? Work? School? Netflix? When you're young it's seemingly easier to get out of bed when the alarm goes off. The world is at your fingertips. Nowadays, it literally is, with smartphones and the like.

There have been numerous times when I've dreaded waking up. Typically, it was due to going to a job I hated. Far fewer people are bummed about waking up on a Saturday (unless they work weekends).

When you go through a few years of life just trying to make it through the day, it starts taking a toll on you. I think I might've actually turned my brain off for a few years in my twenties, just so I wouldn't think about what I was doing. My role as a mindless robot was fulfilled, but unfortunately my passion had dried up.

In all honesty, the jobs weren't that bad, they just weren't fulfilling my passion. Unfortunately, I had no idea what my passion was. But if I had been paying closer attention, I would've known right away.

Hiding in Plain Sight

Every moment of the day I was thinking about writing. I had notebooks, Word documents and scraps of paper filled with ideas for the next piece I was going to write. It consumed me.

I started writing for websites and blogs and have eventually worked myself into a position where I have writing gigs for a few different clients. I'm either lucky, crazy or both, because all of my passions have resulted in ways that I could support myself.

The corporate stuff isn't what gets me out of bed in the morning, though. This does. Writing to you. Sharing my thoughts to hopefully hear yours back someday in whatever form or fashion you choose.

I'm passionate about people, creating things and getting people passionate about creating things.

If you have no idea what I'm talking about, think back to the first time you were in love or had a crush on someone. You wanted to be around them 24/7. You would do anything for them. You couldn't stop thinking about them. Now that's passion.

The funny thing about passion is that it will get you out of bed in the morning, but it'll also keep you up at night. Why sleep when you've finally found your true love?

Passion is Infectious

My favorite thing about passion is that it's contagious. Just watch a passionate person talk about what they're working on—they get so excited that they can barely contain themselves. They just want to share it with the world. Their enthusiasm gets other people excited, and it creates a chain reaction of passion and creativity.

Everyone wants what a passionate person has. We all want purpose. We all want our lives to have meaning. We all want to light up the world.

What are you waiting for?

Hocus Pocus

you need to know is this is your face. This is what you think
you know of it.

These are the three layers of your skin.

These are the three women in your life.

The epidermis, the dermis, and the fat.

Your wife, your daughter, and your mother.

If you're reading this, welcome back to reality. This is
where all the glorious, unlimited potential of your youth
led. All that unfilled promise. Here's what you've done with
your life.

Your name is Peter Wilmot.

All you need to understand is you turned out to be one sorry
sack of shit.

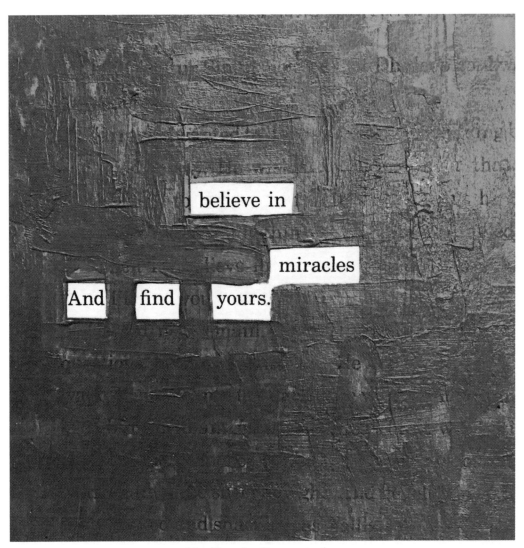

Manifestation Demonstration

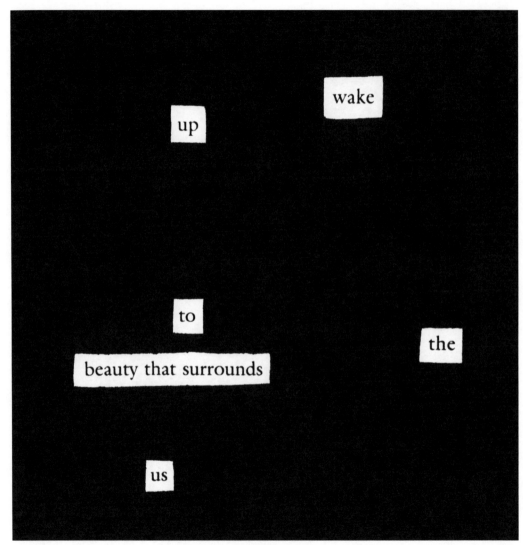

20/20 Vision

Stereotypical Life

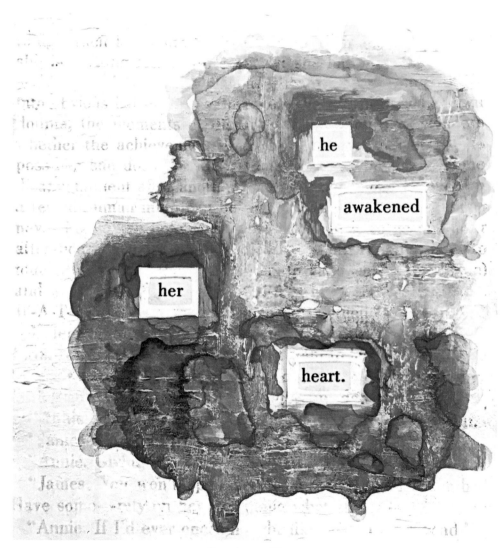

Cognizant of Love

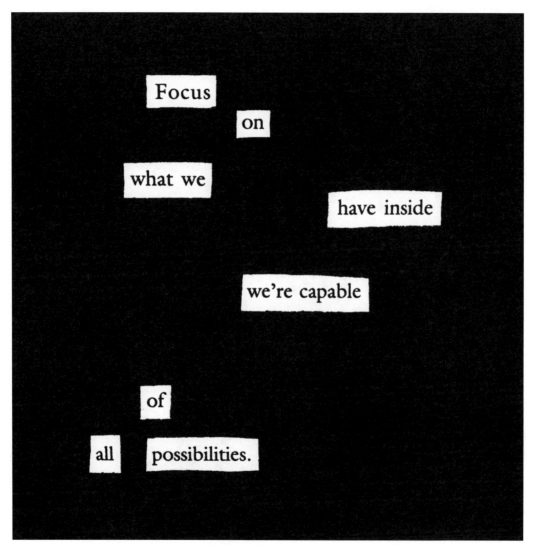

Infinite Potential

enlighten me

whenever possible.

In the Dark

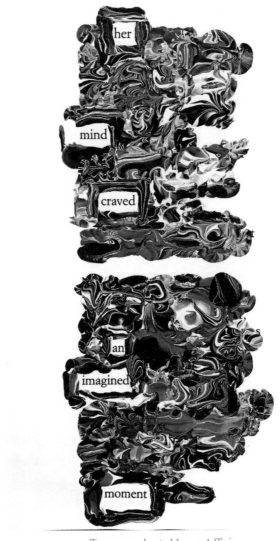

her

mind

craved

an

imagined

moment

Transcendental Love Affair

Fess Up

There is power in the arts.

Create Culture

Change of Heart

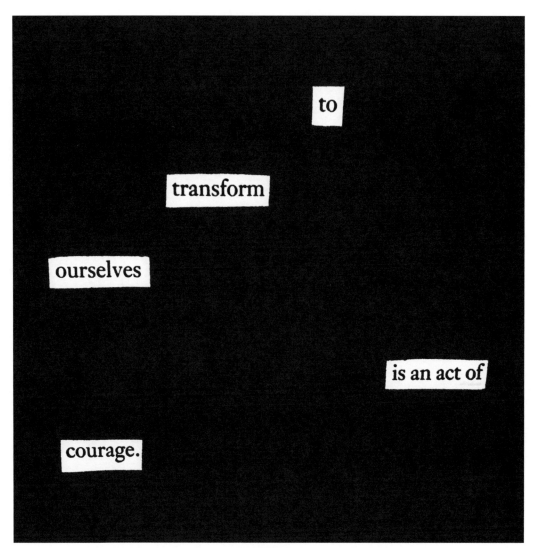

to

transform

ourselves

is an act of

courage.

Heroic Metamorphosis

CREATIVITY

'Creativity is a muscle.'

When I was a kid, I lacked what you would call artistic talent. I had no desire to read books, draw pictures, paint, or even write. My friends would draw Ninja Turtles to pass the time in school while I was too embarrassed to even try. College was off the table because I figured I'd have to write too many papers. In school, if they ever made a reference to creative types, I was on the other side of the room, hiding behind my desk.

So how the hell did I get here?

Finding Your Voice

All creativity starts with a voice. Don't worry if you haven't found yours yet because, fortunately, we all have one. Some are just more developed than others.

But as the subtitle states, creativity is a muscle.

How could you ever write a book if you've never written a sentence? How could you have an art show if you've never painted a picture? How could you ever make a movie if you've never bought a camera? You get the point.

I stumbled upon my voice when blogging first started gaining popularity in the early 2000s. Stuck in a cubicle with four hours of work in an eight-hour day, I decided to start spending my days writing essays and short stories to pass the time. Unknowingly, I was working out my creative muscles.

Finding Your Community

After experimenting with different writing styles for months and creating new entries on a daily basis, I eventually discovered other bloggers who had similar interests. We would comment on each other's posts and give honest feedback. It was a true community. And once I had an audience, I didn't want to stop.

Day after day, I found new ways to challenge myself to keep that audience coming back. It brought me great joy being their audience as well. Our collective passion fueled the community to keep going, to keep creating.

It was a beautiful cycle.

Blogging was pure back then. It's the same with every platform in its infancy stage. Facebook, Instagram and Tumblr all went through the same process. Corporate entities hadn't discovered it yet, and the 'blogosphere' was raw and full of hungry writers wanting to have their work read.

What's amazing about community is that it also sharpens your voice. They'll praise you and rip your work apart, but at the end of the day, it's feedback. Feedback is key when honing your voice.

Finding Your Path

For a long time I bounced around writing essays, short stories, interviews and marketing campaigns for my job, each path leading to a new community. That's the fun of creativity. When you heed the call you never quite know where the path will take you.

On my creative journey, each venture has taught me something new that I can take with me. Writing essays taught me how to explain an idea; journalism educated me on how to introduce a person to the world; fiction was my training ground for storytelling.

Creating Community

Most recently I've landed here, in the blackout poetry community.

Who is this community? It's you, and me, and anyone who ever picks up a marker pen or a paintbrush to make the first of many blackout poetry pieces. This is my favorite community because blackout poetry is for everyone. It's inclusive. All you need is a book, a marker pen, a few minutes and an open mind.

Most people, my former self included, feel like they're not good enough to be an artist, so they never even try. The idea behind Make Blackout Poetry is that everyone is artistic, they just might not know it yet. If creativity is a muscle, then blackout poetry is your five-minute workout plan to unleash inspiration in your mind. It doesn't matter if you're the next Picasso or have never made art in your life, the process is beneficial for everyone.

of interpersonal synergy is embodied in the principles in the first three habits, which give the internal security sufficient to handle the risks of being open and vulnerable. By internalizing those principles, we develop the abundance mentality of Win/Win and the authenticity of Habit 5.

One of the very practical results of being principle centered is that it makes us whole, truly integrated. People who are scripted deeply in logical, verbal, left-brain thinking will discover how totally inadequate that thinking is in solving problems which require a great deal of creativity. They become aware and begin to open up a new script inside. The right brain isn't the right brain wasn't there; it just lay dormant. The muscle had not been developed, or perhaps they had atrophied early in childhood because of the heavy left-brain emphasis of formal education or social scripting.

When a person has access to both the intuitive, creative, and visual right brain, and the analytical, logical, verbal left brain, then the whole brain is working. In other words, there is psychic synergy taking place in our own head. And this tool is best suited to the reality of what life is, because life is not just logical — it is also emotional.

A New Kind of Workout

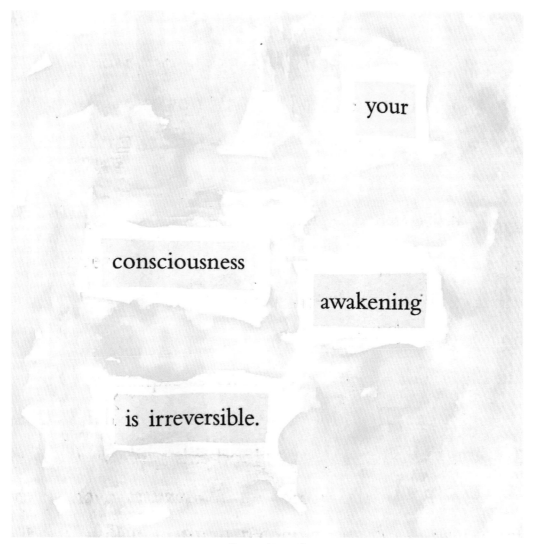

your

consciousness

awakening

is irreversible.

Beyond Recall

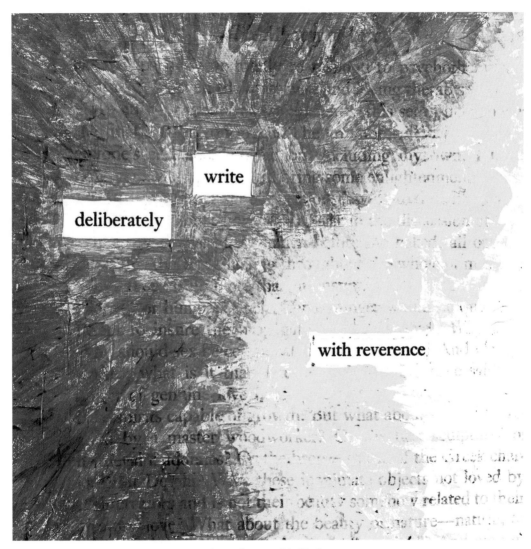

Interchangeable Verb

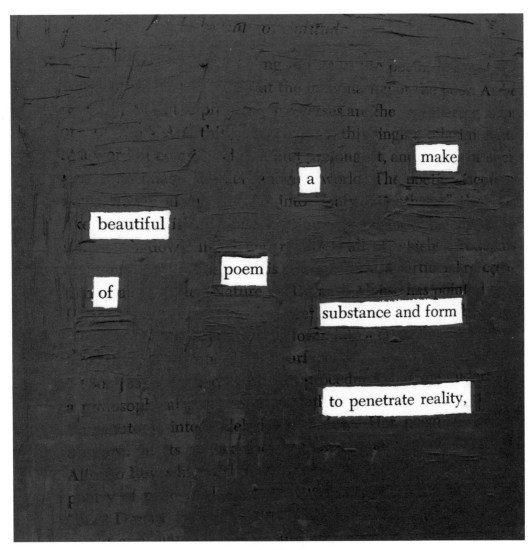

make

beautiful

a

poem

of

substance and form

to penetrate reality,

Magic Words

we're terrified.

we're paralyzed.

something

is

holding us back,

We're just

afraid

of failure

Hesitant Pursuit

don't

fear

Your

idea

ds that kept any-
visual clues, no
to decode just a dog and a bear
being tourists in downtown Seattle.
to expect. Every December, the interna-
tional Society hosts a party called "Santa Rampage"
where hundreds of people come into a city, all of them dressed

Horrific Brilliance

we were born,

creative

So what happened?

Inadvertent Neglect

Infinite Cycle

I found

the only way to escape is

to create

Design Your Freedom

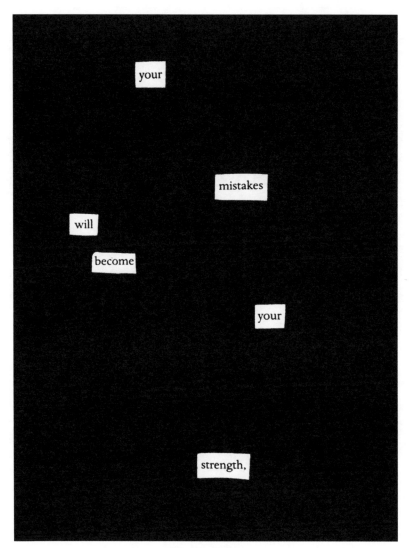

Flip the Script

scrutinize

of those

trying to

found the right

impossible

Negative Connotation

Unobstructed View

CHANGE

'Be the exception.'

Somewhere along the line someone said, *Change is inevitable.* Some lucky guy in the last few hundred years is probably credited with the quote, but it's obviously an ageless truth. Change is based on the decisions and actions of individuals. Nature also takes part by throwing in the unforeseen. Every day we wake up and things are happening around us, and there's nothing we can do to stop it.

This is the inevitability of change at work.

The Choice is Yours

Our choice to play along with these external changes is not required. We can go with the flow or plant our feet firm. Ultimately, internal change is our decision.

Unfortunately, a lot of pain exists in the world as a result of the decision to remain complacent in areas where the universe is nudging us to make a change. We refuse to alter our course and we end up living in the past. Life moves on without us, and we become angry or even depressed because things aren't like they used to be.

The Good Old Days

Another issue that occurs when we reject change is that we often think that our best days are behind us. Whether those were childhood, high school or your college years, it doesn't matter; there's a big world and an amazing life just waiting for you. If you're willing to accept it...

Not to mention, I refuse to believe that anyone's best days are behind them.

Fear of the Unknown

I don't believe that people want to live stagnant lives. They're just afraid. We naturally fear the unknown. It's like learning to swim or ride a bike. We whisper doubt to ourselves, *Everyone else seems to think it's amazing, but what if I fall or sink to the bottom?*

You're not alone. We've all fallen and scraped our knees and struggled in the water gasping for air. That's a part of change, because change is growth. It doesn't always come easy and there's usually a learning curve, but the payoff is worth the pain.

Defining Moment

Imperative Absolution

it
takes
very little effort
to
be a
hero.

No Cape Required

do

little things

for others.

to

change the

world

Compound Effect

...ize how unique they are... ...their task... even though they ...ting, ...materials and insist on all kinds of special ...ment, most of them are happy just to handle the...

Fourth, torchbearers often care more ... **find** ...that they do about which route to take. You ...**solutions.** ...delivery meetings, looking for the perfect... ...real, you'll find them out on the road, pushing their way through ...siders and needs—moving, ...moving, because ...that moving is often the best way **to** ...et where they're going...

Fifth, most important, ...torchbearers don't stop until the ...any torchbearer should ... balance between devotion ...the pursuit of ...A torchbearer never forgets about or ...**change** ...duty, even when there's something...

...you a torchbearer? Probably... ...at challenges... ...Once you've ...in that you ... **the** change **world** will bea... ...of your days...

Collective Effort

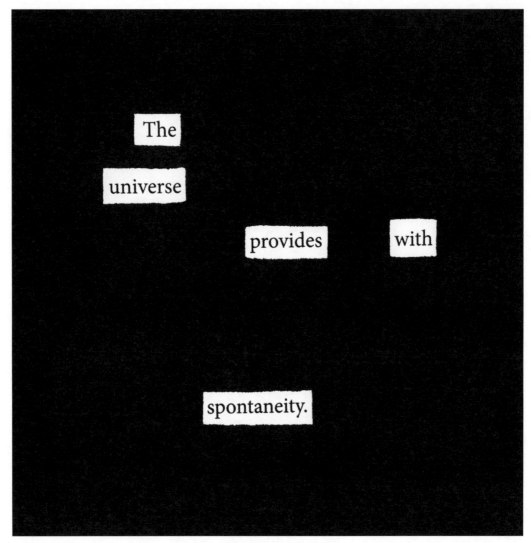

No Coincidence

decide to change the rules

Ratified Amendment

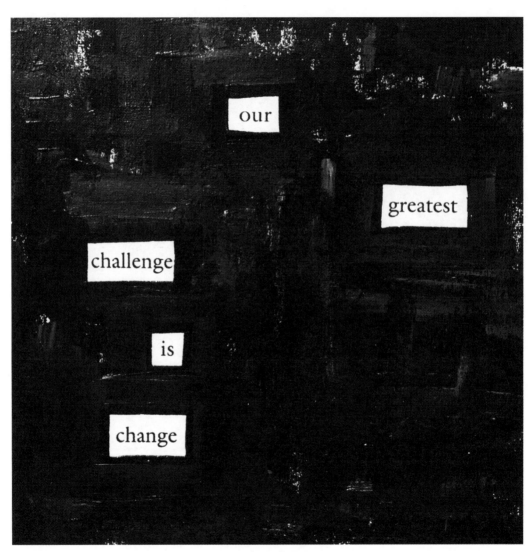

Reversal of Man

Second Opinion

Toxic Threat

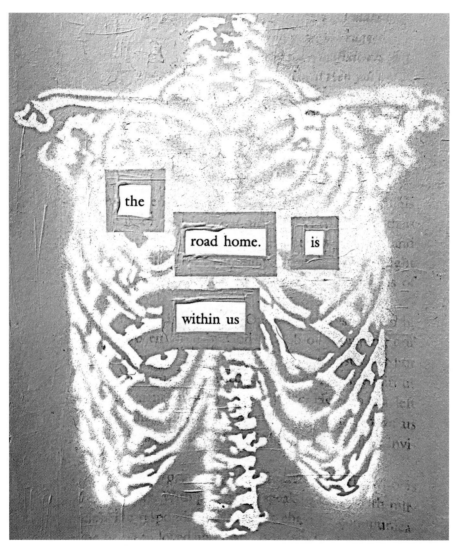

You Are Here

45

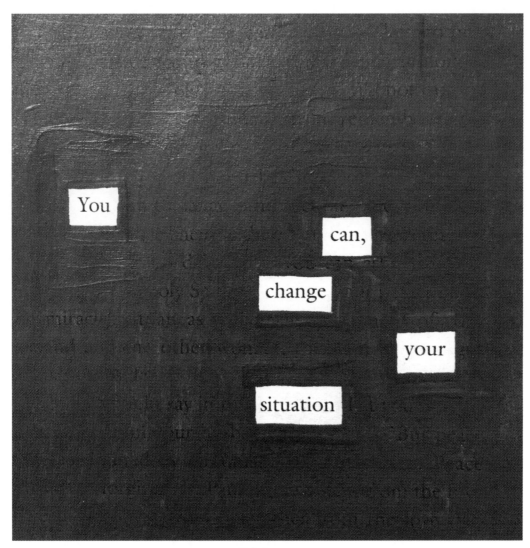

Exit Ramp

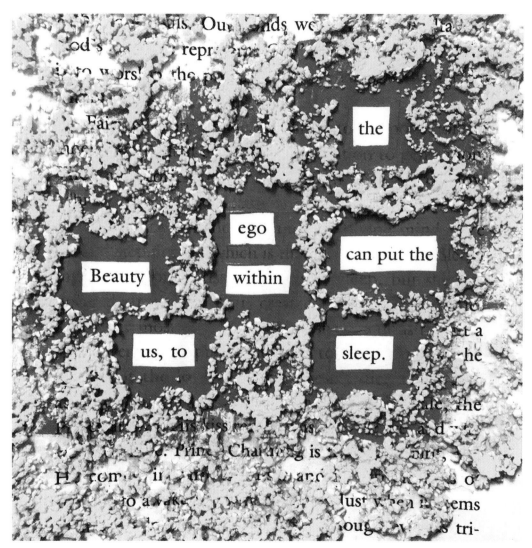

Find Your Way Back

LIFE

'Life is a force without a set course.'

At some point in our lives we've all asked the question, *Why am I here?* People have driven themselves mad trying to figure it out and explain this gigantic mystery. There's probably an aggressive ongoing science vs. religion debate raging in my Facebook feed right now.

If we're honest, we'll probably never know why we exist, so save yourself some time and the headache of pondering our existence. Just because we don't know why we're here on a molecular level doesn't mean we have to live aimlessly, without purpose.

Once we make peace with the universal *why*, it clears up some space to think about the personal aspect of the question. This approach is actually gratifying because we can dictate our *why*. We can be the masters of our fate.

Choose Your Own Adventure

We often forget about our choice—whether it's due to the wear and tear of school, work or our personal lives, our *why* tends to get lost in the shuffle. Then we wake up one day, have a classic freak out moment, and realize that the life we're currently living doesn't even remotely look like our *why*.

Some people are OK with living a life that was predestined for them by their parents, peers or institution of choice. This message is not for those people, but for those who are bored, hungry, depressed and can't sleep at night because they want to get down to the business of *why*. Secretly, I think this message is for everyone, regardless of your upbringing or background.

Day Dreaming

This idea of questioning your *why* may resonate with you, but you have no idea where to start. The beauty of it all is that even thinking about *why* means that you've already begun. Asking is a process and not something that you discover overnight, but the easiest place to start is usually right under your nose with your hobbies or interests.

Maybe you love doing yoga, building websites or cooking in your spare time. You could get your yoga teaching certificate, start a small business to help companies join the 21st century, or you could write a cookbook. The options are endless. So consider what you already find yourself contemplating and realize that you might already know your *why*.

For those of us who can't answer this question within a week or two, I'd encourage you to explore. Try new things. Sign up for a writing workshop, a painting class, the rock climbing gym. And just because your potential *why* doesn't require a small business loan or branding, doesn't mean that it's any less valid.

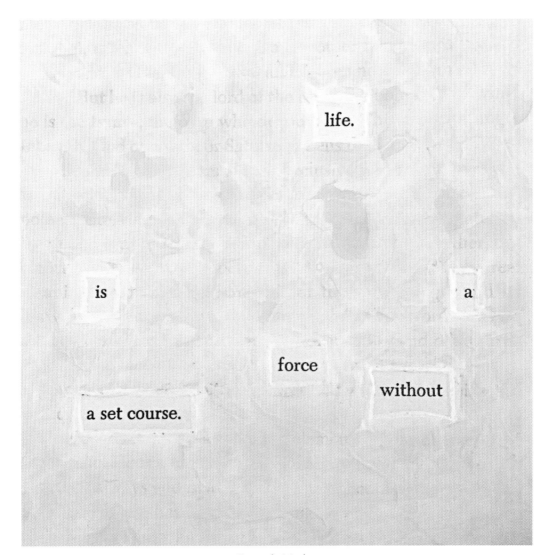

life.

is   a

force

without

a set course.

Ecstatic Motion

the way

live

Beyond

you are

Higher Self

Natural Remedy

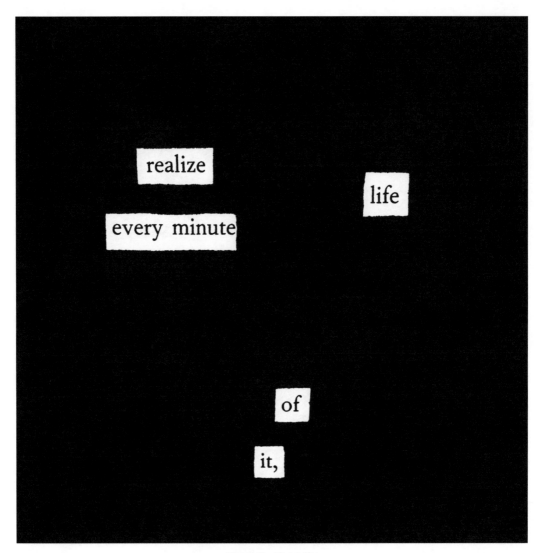

The Mindful Life

believe

in

something that gives you peace.

Transcendental Comprehension

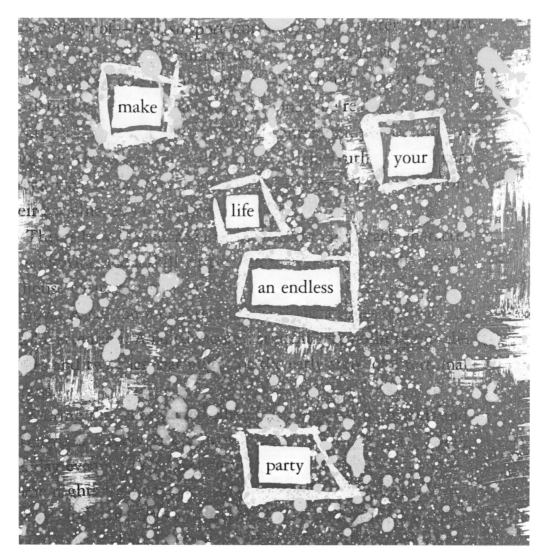

Party Hard

Miracles

will

manifest

if we so desire.

Shift Your Perception

the meaning

of life,

was

Don't be an

asshole

For Future Reference

58

Immaculate Conception

Worth It

LOVE

'We were designed to experience love.'

Some people tend to view love as one of those 'four-letter words' unsuitable for polite conversation. It's jarring, abrupt and powerful. It demands attention.

Our perception of love is a lot like a roller coaster, constantly taking us up and down with its highs and low. After a while, you just want to get off the ride, vowing to never get on again.

Many of us have sworn off love. Maybe even sworn at the idea of it. Once a word of passion, love now brings to mind heartbreak and disgust.

But what if love was more? What if our perception of it was off and we've been looking at it all wrong? What if love was everything that was perfect in the world? What if love was the fabric that held the universe together? What if the Beatles were right and 'all you need is love'?

Fake Love

Humanity has a tendency to use the word love incorrectly.

'I love these shoes.'

'I love Taco Bell.'

'I love that movie.'

'I love you.'

I'm not saying that we don't like our footwear, faux-Mexican fast food, or the latest box office hit, but objects cannot reciprocate love. We especially don't love them after they've been worn out or consumed.

Fake love in relationships is even more detrimental. It's rooted in selfishness and focused on possession and reciprocation. This 'love' comes with terms and conditions.

Real love, though, is unconditional. It doesn't ask for a deposit. It doesn't need to see two forms of ID. It does not require you to sign on the dotted line.

Real Love

Love is all-encompassing.

I believe that everything that is good in this universe was birthed by love. But love is so big that we often don't see it for what it truly is. But when we start to pull back the curtain, we can see love as the orchestrator of all the beautiful instances in our lives.

It's hard to define love, but there's the famously quoted Bible verse you hear at weddings sometimes that says, *Love is patient, love is kind. It does not envy, it does not boast, it is not proud. It is not rude, it is not self-seeking, it is not easily angered, it keeps no record of wrongs.*

If we think about love as being these attributes and actually experience them, we only want more of it. Love is like a tractor beam in *Star Wars*. Once it has you in its grip it's hard to break free.

The Problem

Unfortunately, humanity's choices to not act in love have eroded this world and made us feel like we're second rate citizens; undeserving of love. But why do we hurt others if love feels so good?

Good question. The answer is fear. We fear that we are not loved. We fear that love will not be reciprocated. We fear that we are not worthy of love.

If you look closely, you can easily see that fear breaks the connection of love. We choose not to love, because we fear we will not receive love if we ask for it. In the end, every act of fear is a call for love.

Breaking the Cycle

So how do we fix this? How do we break the cycle of fear? Despite the cliché, how do we make love the answer?

It took me a long time to learn this lesson, but the answer is you. And you. And you, and you. The answer is all of us, individually and ultimately, collectively. If love was a 12-step program, the first step would be learning to love ourselves.

Oscar Wilde said, 'To love oneself is the beginning of a lifelong romance.' The takeaway is, how could we ever love another person, if we don't know how to love ourselves? We have to break the loveless cycle of humanity one person at a time, and to do it, we must start with ourselves.

Self Love

Have you ever held a newborn baby before? Except for crying for food or a diaper change, they're completely happy. No self-deprecating thoughts, no feelings of insecurity, just love. That was all of us, once.

We were brand new. Life hadn't done a number on us. No one had told us that we were ugly. No one had ditched us on prom night. No one had ever bullied us on the Internet. We were pure.

But life kicked in and people mistreated us out of fear of not being loved, which then infected us with the same thought process. And now, here we are. Terrified of love.

For a minute I want you to forget about all of that. I want you to visualize a moment where you felt the most love. Maybe it was a kind word, a long hug, or a selfless act someone made on your behalf. Whatever it was, pause for a moment and go to that place.

That feeling that you just had. The sensation that shot through you. That feeling is what you deserve. This is what you've always been worthy of. The greatest part about that feeling is that once we have it, we want to share it. We literally want to spread the love.

In short, once we learn how to nurture those moments, to create more of them, and learn how to love ourselves, we can start the process of changing the world, one person at a time.

Present Participle

Unlock Your Transformation

Rising Tide

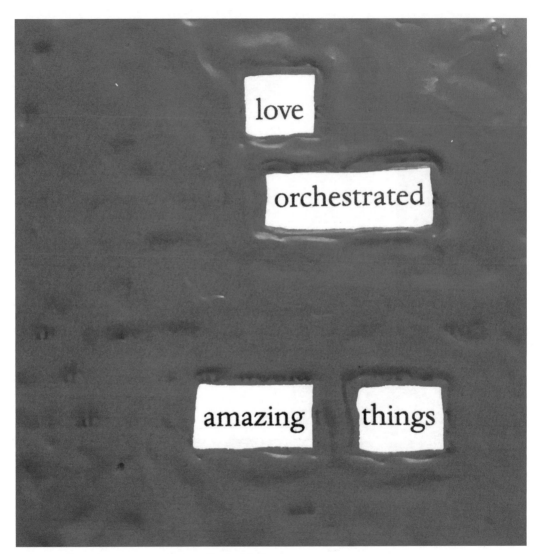

Desirable Arrangement

Instruct My Heart

We

are incapable

of separation from

love.

As Easy to Escape as Your Shadow

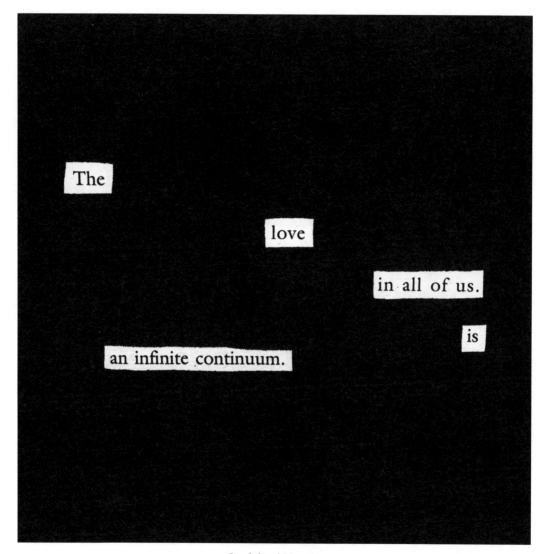

The

love

in all of us.

is

an infinite continuum.

Conjoined Hearts

love

requires

us to simply *be*

Just Relax

Let It Linger

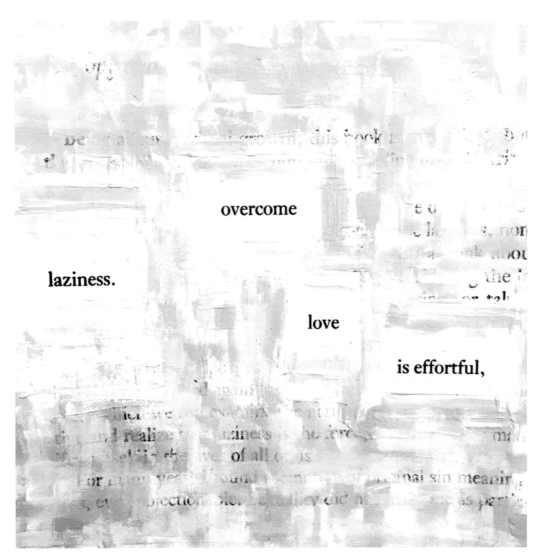

overcome

laziness.

love

is effortful,

Action Required

love

brings us back to

life,

Water Your Soul

Act of Valor

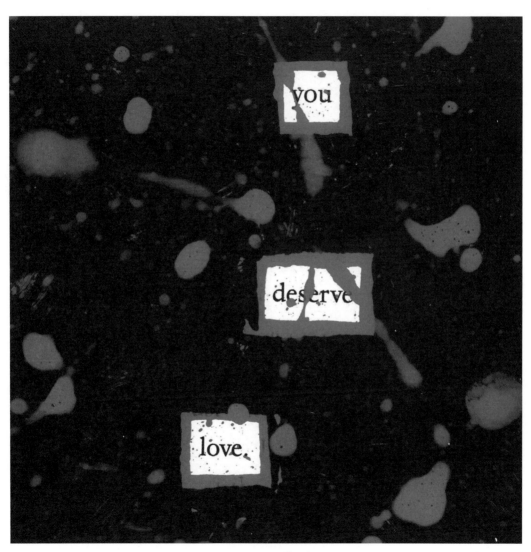

Warranted Affection

Love is
hidden.
within our minds.

Self-Titled

love,
makes it possible
to coexist.

Synchronized Hearts

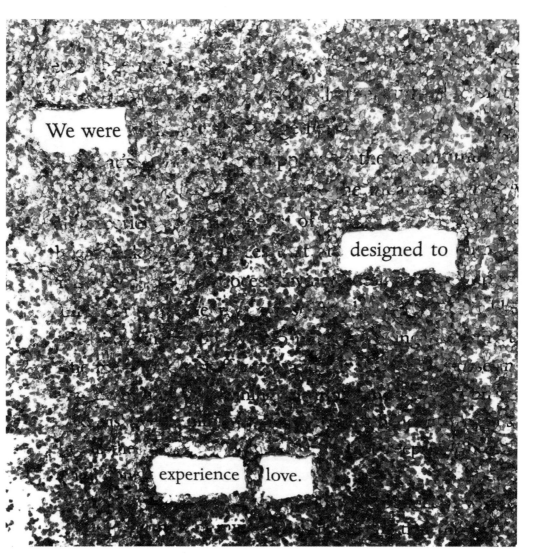

Original Blueprint

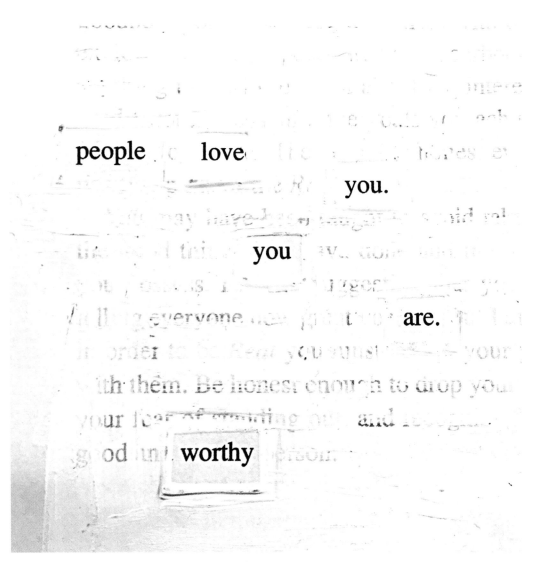

people love you. you are. worthy

Plain & Simple

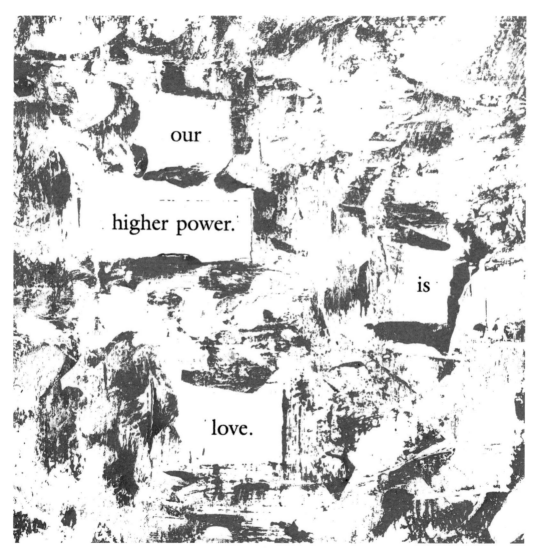

our

higher power.

is

love.

The Indivisible Divine

Be willing to share ~~your product information~~ ~~exactly, first with~~ yourself and then ~~with other~~ ~~people on the mission~~ to find love ~~engage in it~~

Be willing to share yourself and then to find love

DEATH

'Death is only a metaphor, it is not the end.'

When I was 21, my boss had a heart attack at work and died immediately. He was recently married and had a seven-month-old daughter at home. Adam was 27 when he passed away. It was almost the most surreal moment of my life.

The previous year, I was attending an extended outreach program in England. Six weeks into my time there my roommate, who was an avid runner, decided to go for a jog. Within the first mile, he collapsed on the side of the road and passed away.

No warnings. No symptoms. He had a clean bill of health.

Mark was 22 when he took his last breath.

I don't share these stories to spread despair, but to explain my point. Death, though we try to deny that it will ever happen to us, is very real. In this world, death is constant and inevitable. What seems to be the scariest part of death is that we rarely have any idea when we'll hear its knock on our door.

Dying to Live

When I was in high school, I developed anxiety based primarily on the fear of dying. Heights, diseases, even car rides completely terrified me. Every day I thought death was coming for me, but lo and behold, here I sit at age 35, writing this book. I eventually got over my anxiety and decided to live, but I had to get mad first. I'm not sure if that's the right advice to give, but in my case I was sick and tired of wasting my life being afraid of the unknown.

I'm not quite sure if there was an exact moment that I got over my fear or if it was gradual. I just remember having a realization that I was young and potentially had a whole life in front of me, but fear was holding me back.

The Clock is Ticking

Nowadays, I tend to view death as a big clock. I can see the hands and the time passing, but I don't know when it's going to tick its last tock, so to speak. And life is like one of those game shows where you have to complete as many tasks as possible before the time runs out. Pretty terrible metaphors, right? That's just how I see it. We've been given this life and have no clue how long we have, but we have the ability to make the most of it.

What I find interesting about Adam and Mark was that they were both larger-than-life characters. When they walked into a room, they were the guys you wanted to be talking to. They were excited about life and weren't afraid to take advantage of all it had to offer. Though I only knew them for a limited amount of time, I think of them regularly, but I often wonder if they lived every day to its fullest because they knew their time was about to run out.

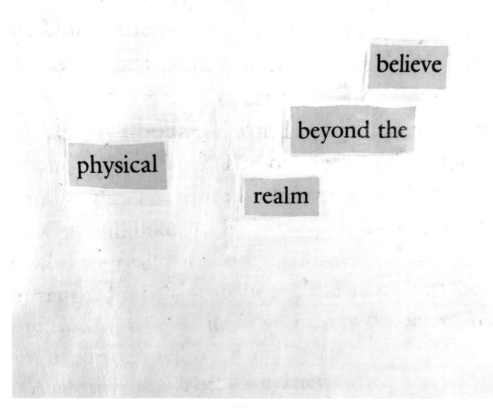

believe

beyond the

physical

realm

Hidden Reality

He touched his hand to his neck
again. "I just felt an emptiness?" He aid this as a quest and Faith
I wanted to be with my family. I
wanted to Olivia

was he one to

worried.

growing up.

about

Lost Boy

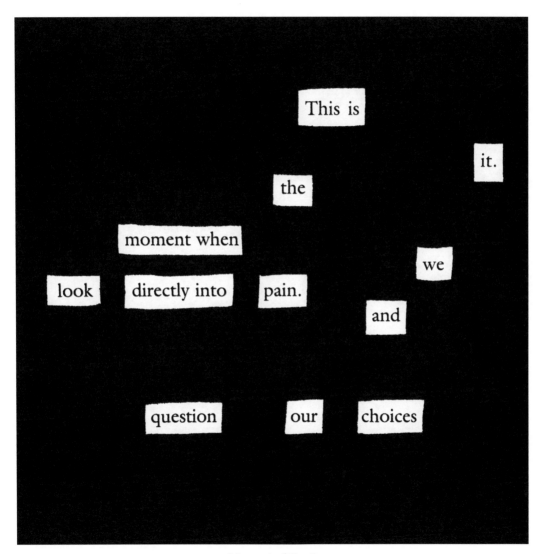

Moment of Truth

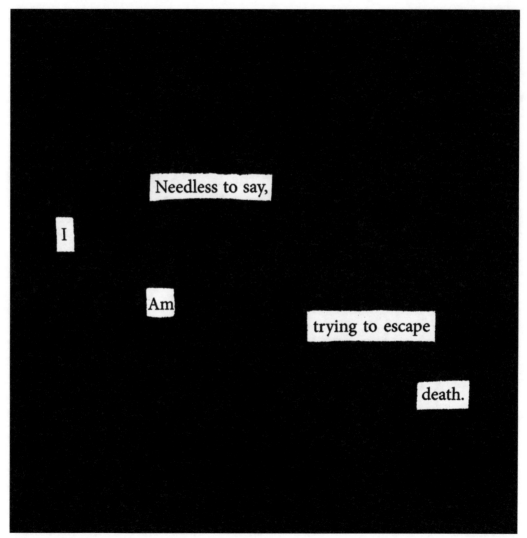

Basic Instinct

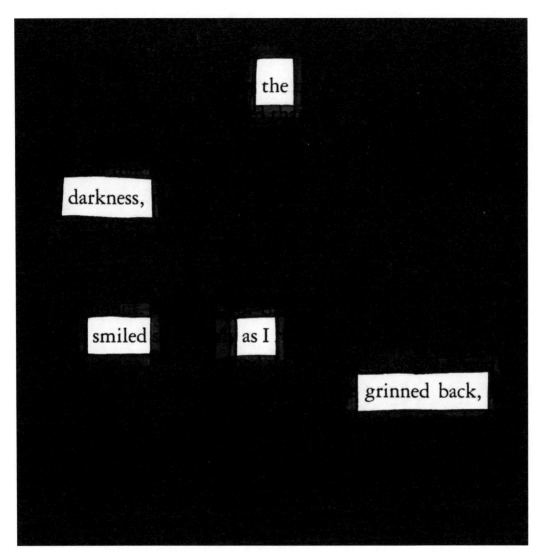

Looking Into the Abyss

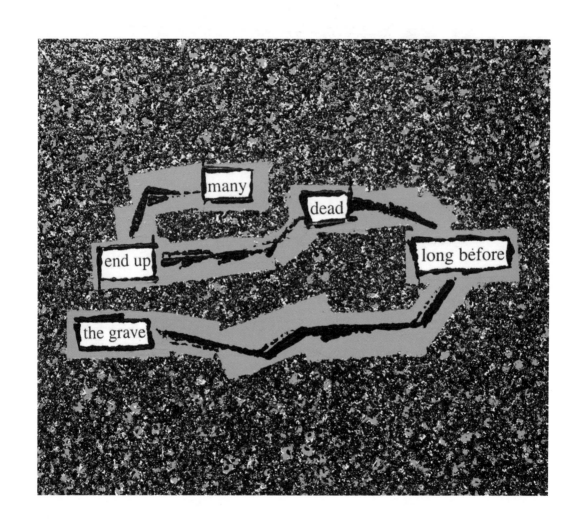

No Signs of Life

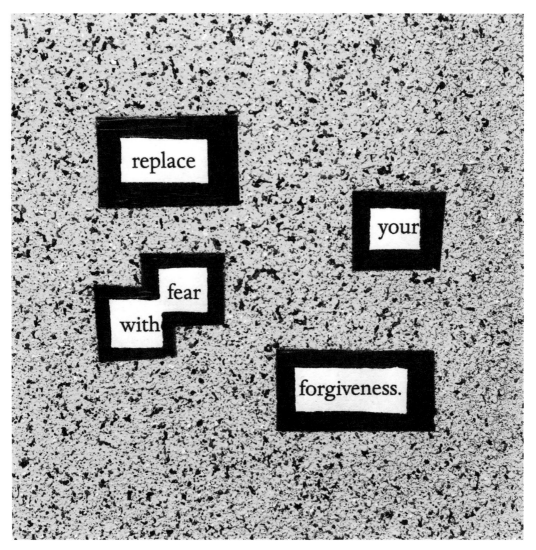

Overhaul Your Heart

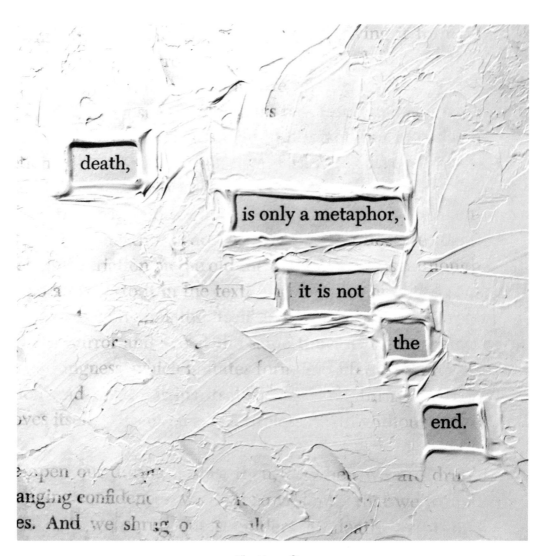

The Hereafter

HOPE

'I unleashed hope and it freed me.'

Hope has an interesting reputation. It's regarded as light and fluffy, but it's anything but. It can be sentimental, inspiring, wishful—it's also excruciating.

Hope is believing the best in a godawful situation. Hope is choosing to hang on just a little bit longer when you feel like you have nothing to live for. Hope is putting down the bottle, deciding to stay, deciding to leave, not pulling the trigger.

Hope is a Choice

It's gritty, painful and not easily stomached. That's why so many people choose despair. It's easy to be a pessimist. It's easy to give up. It's easy to not believe in something better. Hope may be agonizing, but it's also brave, and it takes courage.

I remember when I made the decision to hope.

Working a dead end job. Living paycheck to paycheck. A broken heart with a messy mind.

I wanted to do something. Make a difference. Leave my mark. But what?

The complete unknown can be a frightening thought, but with the right perception it can also be exhilarating. In my situation, it would've been easy to just curl up in a ball and call it quits, but hope wouldn't let me.

I knew it had to get better, but it couldn't unless I pressed on. Ultimately, I realized that the unknown partnered with hope leads to an exciting life. No longer mundane and boring, every day is like one of those *Choose Your Own Adventure* books that I read when I was a kid.

Hope is a Verb

Sometimes life doesn't work out the way we want, the way we hoped for. Even when faced with an outcome that falls flat, the process of hope still changes you. It shows us that we can believe in something better, that we can believe in ourselves.

Life is a process. Regardless of what others may say, it's not about the destination. It's about the choices and experiences that shape who we are and the lives we live.

We will arrive at our destination when we're supposed to, and sooner than we think. But it's more important who we arrive as. And just remember, when life is at its darkest, hope is the companion that leads us home.

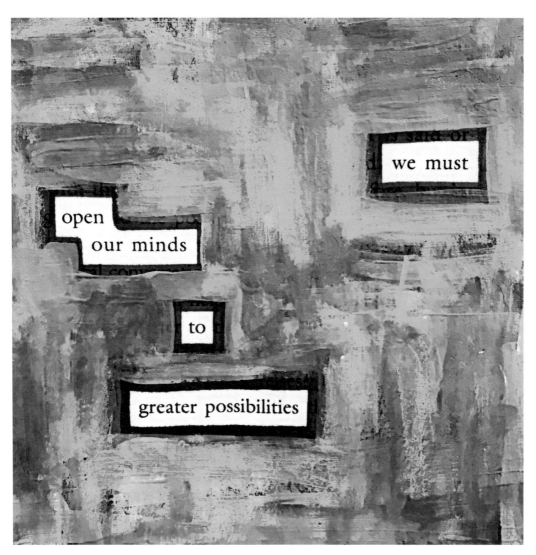

Empirical Probability

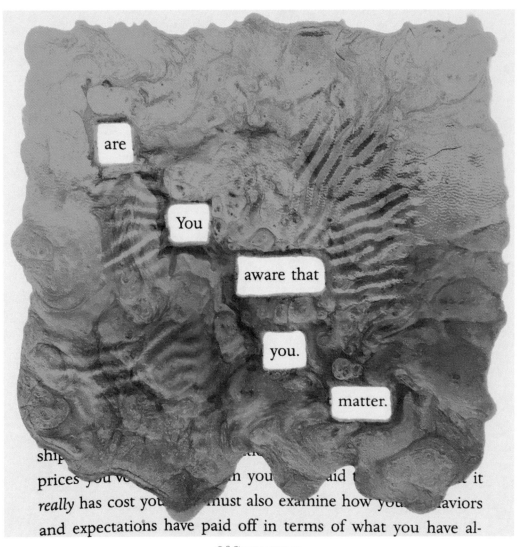

are

You

aware that

you.

matter.

ship
prices you ve ... n you ... aid t ... it
really has cost you ... must also examine how you ... aviors
and expectations have paid off in terms of what you have al-

Of Consequence

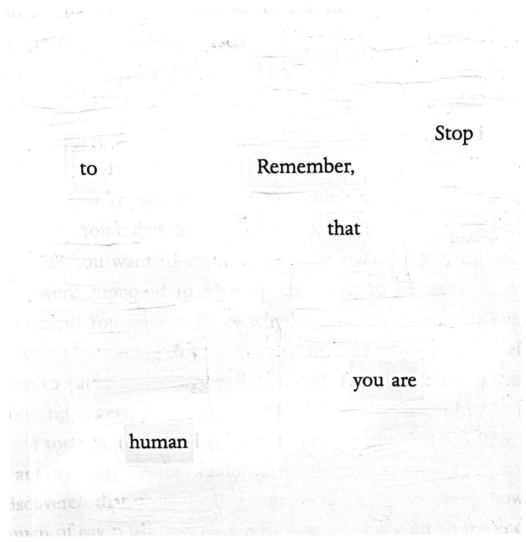

Stop

to   Remember,

that

you are

human

Off the Hook

True North

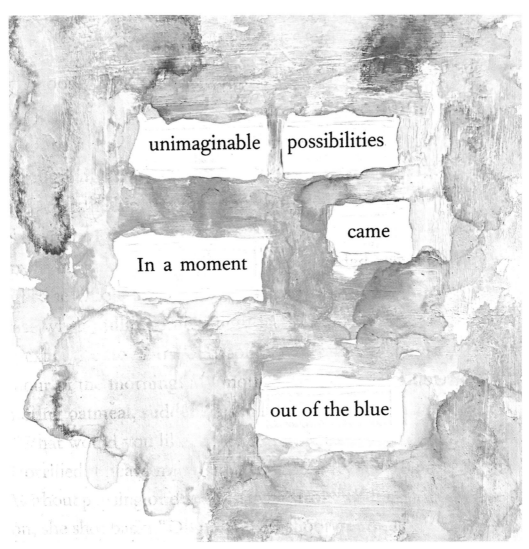

Miraculous Intervention

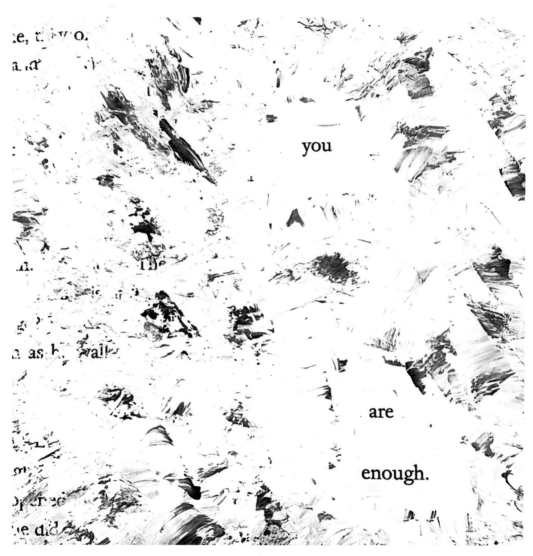

you

are

enough.

Only You

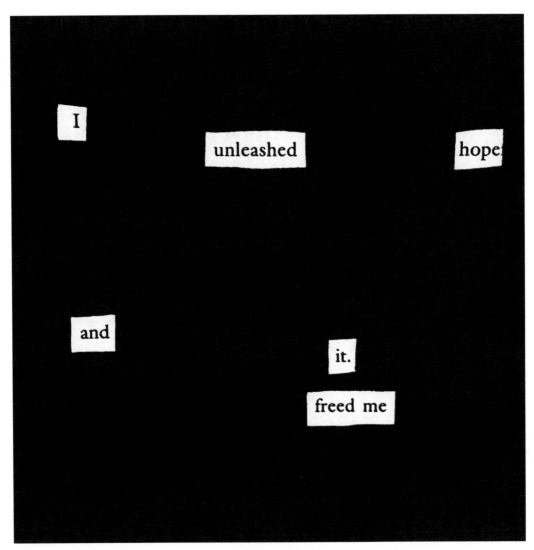

Prison Break

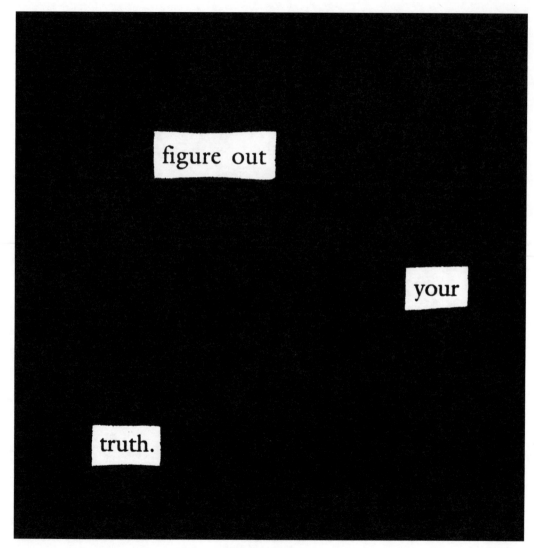

figure out

your

truth.

The Search is On

Unexpected Turbulence

What's Yours?

ABOUT THE AUTHOR

John Carroll is a writer and artist from Atlanta, Georgia.

He is the founder of Make Blackout Poetry.

You can connect with him at
www.makeblackoutpoetry.com.

Follow him on Instagram at @makeblackoutpoetry.

Share your blackout poetry with him on Instagram by using the hashtag
#makeblackoutpoetry.

Thank you to the following people for constantly believing in me, even when I started destroying books with a Sharpie marker:

Patrick Carroll, Reba Carroll, Ray Geier, Jon Walker, and Joel Cantrell.

Thank you to Amy King, Laura Relyea, and Mike Germon for supporting me on this journey.

Thank you to Eyewear Publishing, Alexandra Payne, Deer Bear Wolf, Matt DeBenedictis, Jessica Hunt, Ray Geier, and Brian Manley for making this book a reality.

Last, but not least, thank you to everyone who has ever 'liked', shared, retweeted, reblogged, reposted, or purchased any piece of my blackout poetry. None of this would exist without you.

Please note, I have used "American" spelling in this book. That's the language I use and know. I hope my readers in other parts of the world, including the UK and Ireland, will understand.